my
missmatched
life

a maRvelOus, zAnY, kOoky,
fAbuLOus sCrApBoOk

CHRONICLE BOOKS

ISBN 0-8118-5108-7

Design by Anna Sorkina.
Typeset in Gill Sans.
Manufactured in China.

Distributed in Canada by
Raincoast Books
9050 Shaughnessy Street
Vancouver, British Columbia V6P 6E5

10 9 8 7 6 5 4 3 2 1

Chronicle Books LLC
85 Second Street
San Francisco, California 94105
www.chroniclebooks.com

Chronicle Books endeavors to use environmentally responsible
paper in its gift and stationery products.

LighTs! cOLoRs! aCtiOn! If life is a movie, then yours is a big-budget action adventure. You do the unexpected. You stand out. You do things that are daring, fun, and just **tOTaLLy yOU**. Welcome to your marvelous, zany, kooky, fabulous, missmatched life!

Being a **miSsMatcHed** girl means not matching everyone else. Living a missmatched life means seeing and **dOiNg tHiNGs difFeREntLy**. It means being creative and energetic—and **LiViNG tO The fULL-eSt**. You like to do things upside down, backwards, and sideways. Whether you're kinda, sorta, alota, or **tOTaLLy** missmatched is up to you.

hOw miSsMatcHed aRE yOU? Use this book to find out. Fill this **sCRapbOOk** with stories and art to record anything and everything about your friendships, fashion quirks, pets, family, travel, dreams, and **sEcret deSirEs**. Make this scrapbook a place where you can **tHinK biG**, play with ideas, and record your memorable life.

In this scrapbook, feel free to **miX iT uP!** Gather plane tickets, ticket stubs from your favorite movies, locks of hair, **BubBLe gUm** wrappers, horoscopes, **fORtuNe-cOOkiE fORtuNes**, report cards, notes from friends, and **anYtHiNG** else that catches your eye. Go through old photo albums and **piCk oUT YoUR WeiRdeSt**, wackiest, most missmatched photos—or if you can, start carrying around a **cAMERa** to take new ones. Be sure to check out the "**miX iT uP!**" activities. If you want to do 'em instead, that's great. You also might want to start writing down **yOUR dReaMs**, daydreams, hopes, fears, and anything that maaaaaakes youuuuuuuu maaaaaaaaaaaaaaaad! You're going to use all of these things to create the **cOoleSt** and **mOst miSsMatcHed** scrapbook **in hiStoRy!!!**

sCRaPbOOkiBleS

Okay, here's how to celebrate your fabulous life the missmatched way: You are now officially crowned Scrapbook Queen. Start by flexing your imagination. Collect all kinds of things that you can glue, tape, and staple into this book. If you find things that aren't flat or small enough to fit in here—like a gummy bear or a poster of your favorite singer—figure out if you can flatten them or make them smaller. Below are some fun ideas of things to collect and paste, as well as some suggestions for tools you'll need to help you record your marvelous, zany, kooky, fabulous, missmatched life!

☆ Pens and markers in all colors

♡ Scissors

❀ Camera

○ Glue sticks

☆ Tape

♡ Paintbrushes

❀ Crayons

○ Acrylic paint

☆ Photo corners

❀ Rubber stamps

○ Stickers with fun words and pictures

  (Some are enclosed to get you started!)

☆ Magazines and newspapers

♡ Colorful ribbons for borders

❀ Glitter (for your glittery life)

○ Stickers, stickers, and more stickers

☆ Did I mention stickers?

♡ Washable-ink ink pads

miX iT uP!

Do you know any friends or famous people who were born on the same day as you? Paste (or draw) their pictures and write down their names. How do you match or missmatch?

a FeW oF mY fAvORite cRazY tHingS

Maybe it's your bright orange hairbrush, your constantly shedding dog, your tuba, or your soccer ball. Take photographs of all the things you love—your favorite CDs, cars, hair-styles, and anything else that you're crazy about—or cut out pictures from catalogs and magazines and paste them here. If your favorite color is lime green, cover this page with pieces of lime-green fabric and pictures of funky lime-green stuff. If you love dogs, draw a picture of your dog (if you have one) and tape a tiny piece of her hair here!

fAbuLOus foOdS

Which foods do you love and which ones gross you out? What are your best friend's favorite foods? Make a chart of who likes what. Or make a collage of your favorite foods using labels, photos, and whatever else you can find. Better yet, don't buy it—cook it! Do you know someone who makes the best chocolate-chip cookies or potato salad in the world? Ask him or her to write the recipe on an index card (one side only), and paste it here.

m¡X iT uP!

What's the weirdest food combination you like to eat? Dark chocolate with potato chips? Mayonnaise-and-peanut-butter sandwiches with lettuce and tomato? Do you love watermelon with salt? Keep a freaky food log here.

mY mIssmAtcHeD fAMilY

Make a list (oldest to youngest) of your grandparents, parents, aunts, uncles, brothers, sisters, and other relatives. Take pictures of them and glue the photos next to their names. For relatives who don't live nearby, gather pictures you have of them from vacations and other get-togethers. If you can't find a current picture of someone, attach his or her baby picture or draw a portrait. And, just for fun, next to each relative's name and photo, glue pictures of things that remind you of him or her. For example, if your Aunt May makes the best blueberry pie ever, paste a picture of one by her name. Yum!

m¡X iT uP!

To add to the insanity, think about what animal each family member would be if he or she were an animal. Cut out a picture of the animal and put it on one side of your relative's head.

hOlidAy MaDneSs

What are your favorite holidays? Find pictures of your favorite Halloween costumes, Christmas trees, that silly hat you wore for New Year's Eve, and other images from your favorite celebrations. Now capture and personalize these memories: If your favorite holiday is Halloween, grab a marker and draw that cute costume you wore in the space below, and write down why it was so cool. If you love Valentine's Day, make a collage from old valentines and rank their senders on a scale from 1 (No way!) to 10 (In my dreams!). Or outline a Christmas tree, a menorah, a heart, or any other shape that relates to a favorite holiday and fill the outlines with holiday memories.

miX iT uP!

Mix and match holidays with a collage!
Decorate a Christmas tree with
Valentine's Day hearts. Design
a Halloween-Thanksgiving
costume—how would you
dress up like a turkey?

tHe pEt fiLEs

Of course your pet is the smartest, funniest, cutest animal on the planet. Draw or paste a picture of him or her doing all the fun pet things like eating, sleeping, and smiling. Next to the montage, write your pet's autobiography: Where was he born? Do you know your pet's pet peeves? What is your pet's funniest trick?

mｉX iT uP!

If you don't have a pet, make one up. Cut up pictures from wildlife and pet magazines and make your own breeds of mixed-up animals. What would a lion-dog, a dragon-rabbit, or a caterpillar-parakeet look like?

miX iT uP!

Ask friends and family members to send you letters in envelopes with fun stamps. Cut out and paste your favorite stamps here.

YoUr rAvishiNg rOom

You have your very own, unique sense of style. You're you, and no one else in the world is the same. Does your room reflect your dynamic personality? Use this page to describe how: Take pictures of your room and list everything you like about it. What color is your comforter? What pictures or posters hang on your walls? What does your room say about you?

m¡X iT uP!

Would you give your room a makeover if you could?
Cut out pictures of things you'd love to have in
your room. Would you paint the walls sea blue?
Would you add fluffy pillows or a funky
lamp? Do you like to missmatch
your colors to spice
things up?

hoW dOes YoUR gArdeN gRoW?

Flowers decorate the world. Now you can make pressed flowers to decorate YOUR world—and this scrapbook. Other decorations from the natural world: Glue pebbles from the park, or make a sidewalk rubbing or a plant print. If you don't have a garden, you can do this at your favorite park.

✿ To press flowers, place the flower between two sheets of paper and press between two heavy books (dictionaries and phone books work very well for this) for two weeks. You can seal the flowers between layers of clear contact paper to help the flowers retain their color a little longer.

✿ To press leaves, place the leaves between two pieces of wax paper and cover the wax paper with two layers of newspaper. Ask a grown-up to iron the newspaper for a minute or two on low until the wax melts and seals the leaves.

✿ To make a sidewalk rubbing, place a sheet of plain white paper over a leaf or anything lying on the sidewalk. Peel the label off a crayon, and rub the long side of it back and forth over the paper until you can see the shape of the object.

eXtrEMe sPorTS

If you could invent an Olympic sport, what would it be? Snowshoe bowling? Soccer ballet? Hip-hop checkers? Make up the rules and write them down here. For example, for soccer ballet, you have to twirl twice before you kick the ball. For hip-hop checkers, you have to bust a move before you can move your piece.

m¡X iT uP!

Do you play a sport? Paste pictures of you and your team here. Jot down everything you remember about the best plays you ever made, or write in the names of your favorite sports teams and athletes, along with pictures of them cut out from magazines and newspapers.

mAd FoR MoVies

Do you love to sit in a darkened theater and watch a story unfold? Start collecting the ticket stubs from your favorite movies—and the ones that totally bombed! Paste the stubs here and write a mini-review underneath.

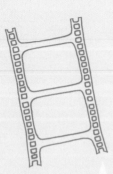

miX iT uP!

If you were to make a movie, what would it be about? Would it be a sci-fi thriller love story about a pack of puppies lost on Mars? Or would it be the movie version of your life? Make a list of all the key players in your life and then write down your casting choice next to each name.

tHe sOunDs oF MuSic

Make a list of your favorite singers, bands, and songs. Now arrange them here in order of preference to create your all-time favorite playlist. If you were going to make the perfect CD, what songs would you include on it? What lyrics so closely match your lifestyle that they could be your personal theme song?

m¡X iT uP!

Write a song about something that's going on in your life. Sometimes a song comes from a single line. Next time someone says something funny or memorable to you, use it as the first line for your song. Another way to write a song is to copy your favorite lines from different songs and then rearrange them on the page to make a whole new song.

nEigHboRhoOd wAtcH

Do you know all the people in your neighborhood? Take a walk around your block and draw pictures or take photos of the trees, shops, flowers, cars, and neighbors you see. Paste the photos or drawings below, along with short descriptions or stories about them. What do you love about the place where you live?

Name:_____

Birthday:_____

Sign:_____

Nickname:_____

Favorite outfit:_____

Favorite movie star:_____

Favorite food:_____

Best talent:_____

Our favorite saying is:_____

The thing I like about him/her the most:_____

_____

Name:_____

Birthday:_____

Sign:_____

Nickname:_____

Favorite outfit:_____

Favorite movie star:_____

Favorite food:_____

Best talent:_____

Our favorite saying is:_____

The thing I like about him/her the most:_____

_____

fRieNdly iNTerVieWs

Now it's time to tell all! Imagine that you are writing a celebrity profile of your best friend for your favorite magazine. Interview your friend and then your friend can interview you. What would you tell your fans about yourselves? Here are some questions to get you started. You can ask and answer more questions on the next page.

What makes you totally you? _____

_____

What was the weirdest day of your life? _____

_____

What is the funkiest, most original thing you wear? _____

_____

If you were stranded on a deserted island, what three people would you take with you?

_____

mｉX ｉT uP!

Swap scrapbooks and have your
friend write your biography
in your book and you
can write her biography
in hers.

fUnkY fiNgERpriNts

Like snowflakes, no two people's fingerprints are alike. Get ink pads in different colors. Press each finger on the ink pad and then gently roll it onto the page. Now have all your friends and family do the same thing. Write each person's name next to his or her prints.

mɪX ɪT uP!

For extra fun, you can create your own animals out of fingerprints. When you draw ears, a nose, beak, whiskers, or a tail, your thumbprint becomes an owl, or a cat, or a dog. Mix and match your fingerprints with your friend's to see what else you can make.

hAir tOdAy, gOne ToMorRow

Okay, so we've all had some fab hairdos and a few serious hair-don'ts! Here's a place for you and your friends to play with your hair and record all of your stylish creations. All you need is a camera, some cute hair ties, and bright barrettes. For inspiration, page through style magazines. If you see fun 'dos you'd like to try, clip out the pictures and paste them here—along with photos of how the styles look on you.

Here are a few more ideas for things to mix and match in your new hairdos:

♡ Beadazzled: **Look for colorful beads and string them on pieces of elastic (available at craft or fabric stores) to create beaded ties. Use the ties at the ends of your braids or ponytails.**

♡ Rainbows of ribbons: **Braid ribbons of different colors into your hair.**

♡ 1,001 braids: **The next best thing to cornrows. See how many little braids or tiny ponytails you can make in your hair.**

♡ Ballerina buns: **Pull your hair back into a fabulous bun—or two or three. Use colorful bobby pins to slick back your hair.**

♡ Butterfly barrettes: **For a short, perky 'do, dot your hair with tiny barrettes.**

oUTRaGeOUs oUtfiTs

Ever wonder just what you would look like sporting an out-of-this-world hat or decadent 'do that you've seen in a magazine? Now's your time to find out. First, take photos of yourself in your most outrageous outfits. Next, cut and paste on different hairdos and hats from magazines or use the stickers included (the wackier the better). How do you look with a mohawk? Maybe your favorite look is you with red hair in an evening gown?

m¡X iT uP!

Create a collage by cutting pictures
out of magazines and catalogs. Include a head
cut out from one place, a totally terrific
top from another, and a dazzling
skirt from a third and put
them all together. Mix and
match—and voilà!

miX'n'mAtch fRieNdS

Are your best friend and you so alike that sometimes you forget who's who? Take a picture of her against a colorful wall and have her take a picture of you against another wall. Cut out your heads and rearrange them on each other's bodies. So weird!

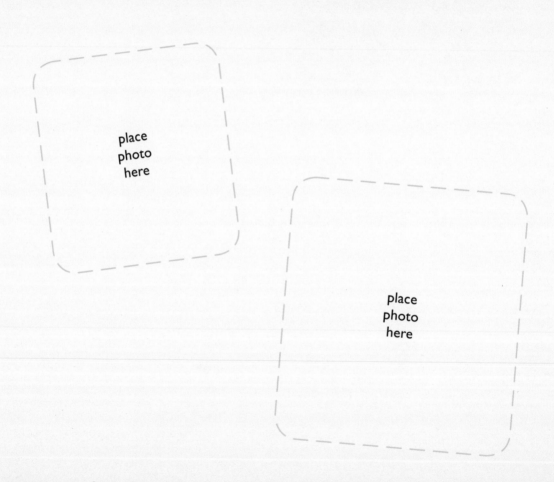

place
photo
here

place
photo
here

eXceLLent aDveNtuRe

Make a collage of the most excellent trip or outing you've ever taken. Did you travel to Paris or Mexico City, or not so far away—the beach, an amusement park, or the zoo? Were you stuck in the back seat of the car for the entire trip, or did you fly by yourself? Here's the perfect place to make a collage of all the highs and lows of your adventure. Glue in maps, ticket stubs, and photos of yourself on your trip. Write about the people you met, the sights you saw, and the food you ate. Where do you want to go next?

siGn o' tHe tiMes

What's in your future? Everything wonderful, no doubt! Will you be President? Buy a horse? Check and see. Paste telling horoscopes and fortune-cookie fortunes here. Looking over them all, do you spot any trends? Are you going to find true love? What are your lucky numbers? Do you have lucky days ahead?

stRaNge DrEAms

Wake up! Wake up! Wake up! Now hold on to that dream! Were you just soaring through the sky? Or suddenly naked at school while giving a book report? Arrrgh! Write down your dreams every morning for a week on a separate piece of paper. Then take out the strangest parts and paste them here. What do you think they mean?

m¡X iT uP!

Illustrate your dream adventures by
covering the page with photos from
magazines to create a dream collage,
or draw a picture or cartoon that
sums up what happened to
your sleeping self.

tiMe cApsUle

What do you want to remember from this amazing moment in time? Gather some of your favorite memorabilia and create a time capsule of your life—right in this book. Paste in everything—from a lock of your hair to a photocopy of the liner notes from your favorite CD. Be creative! How about writing the headlines from the news for the next month? If you want to jot down some notes about the here and now, here are a few questions to get you started:

☆ Who is your favorite pop star or movie actor?

☆ What are the top three things you and your friends talk about?

☆ What is the biggest fashion trend at your school?

☆ What is the most stylish color? (Is brown the new black? Pink the new orange? Do tell . . .)

dReAmY sTuFf

There are all kinds of fun things out there we'd like to have: a new hat, a cat, world peace, a party! If you won the lottery and went on a massive shopping spree, what would you do with all your loot? After all, a girl can dream, right?

a WiSH foR tHe WoRLd

Do you have a dream for the world? How about peace, love, harmony, and ice cream for lunch every day? Imagine the world the way you'd like it to be and cut out pictures to make a dream-world collage. What can you do to make these dreams happen? Is there one small, unexpected, missmatched thing you can do today for someone you know? Examples:

○ Send a postcard to a friend

○ Plant flower seeds in a field

○ Say something nice to your pesky little brother or sister

○ Call a family member who is far away

OfF tHe cHArt!

stick these on the corners of your pictures!

ThE nEw Us

mY wAy

aLOta_____

kiNDa_____

tHe nEw mE

sAsSy

oUttA cONtRoL!

tOP sECReT

cAn't LiVE witHOuT iT!

tOtaLLy oRigiNaL

chANgE tHE wOrLd

sOrtA_____